SOUTHWARK, BERMONDSEY & ROTHERHITHE

A SECOND SELECTION

STEPHEN HUMPHREY

SUTTON PUBLISHING LIMITED

Sutton Publishing Limited
Phoenix Mill · Thrupp · Stroud
Gloucestershire · GL5 2BU

First published 1997

Copyright © Stephen Humphrey, 1997

British Library Cataloguing in Publication Data
A catalogue record for this book is available from the
British Library.

ISBN 0-7509-1577-3

Typeset in 10/12 Perpetua.
Typesetting and origination by
Sutton Publishing Limited.
Printed in Great Britain by
Ebenezer Baylis, Worcester.

ACKNOWLEDGEMENTS

Acknowledgement is gladly made to Mr C. Rumbold, who made an excellent photographic survey of Bermondsey in 1976, for his agreeing to my use of the views of Courage's Brewery on page 19 and of 41 Rotherhithe Street on page 74; to Mr J.H. Warbis for the use of the picture of Borough High Street on page 9; to Major J.M.A. Tamplin for his kind permission to let me use the photographs on pages 112, 113 and 114, all of which relate to the 24th Battalion, the London Regiment (The Queen's); and to Mr Daniel Dougherty for allowing me to reproduce the Melior Street School view on page 34 and the Guy Street Jubilee picture on page 126. The rest of the illustrations belong to the Southwark Local Studies Library and are used by kind permission of Mrs Janice Brooker, Local Studies Librarian in 1994–5, and of her successor, Mr Len Reilly. I would also like to thank Dr Peter Renton for giving me valuable information on synagogues; Mr Roy Bendrey for bringing many matters of local interest to my attention; and Mr Peter Gurnett for much helpful advice on Rotherhithe and the Thames.

CONTENTS

No. 4 Green Dragon Court, Borough Market, *c.* 1930. In 1923 a local businessman, Robert Frank, brought a seventeenth-century doorway and two pilasters from Middleburg in Holland and used them to adorn a rather nondescript house in this alley next to the Borough Market. Before very long a myth had grown up that the house was ancient and special, and even Queen Mary ventured to inspect it. The real story was fortunately published and the myth squashed, but the case shows how easily a totally inaccurate version of history can become established.

INTRODUCTION

This book consists of 191 photographs of the historic district of Southwark, which faces the City of London across the Thames, and of Bermondsey, its downstream neighbour, which was once an important industrial area and a significant part of the Port of London.

Southwark's proud history stretches back to Roman times, when it was London's first suburb, as a result of its being at the southern end of a river crossing. That crossing was revived and fortified by English kings in the ninth century: either then or later it became the London Bridge of recorded history. It was that bridge, the only one in central London until 1750, which made Southwark a focus for travellers from south-east England and therefore a place famous for its inns. Chaucer, Shakespeare and Dickens all refer to Southwark's inns in their works. Shakespeare had a close relationship with Southwark, as part-owner of the Globe Theatre near Park Street, where many of his most famous plays were first performed, and probably as a resident. Dickens knew Southwark well from his father's days in the Marshalsea Prison.

By Dickens's time, Southwark and Bermondsey were populous manufacturing and commercial districts, in which leather tanning, engineering, brewing, food processing, the hop and timber trades, and cargo-handling were all prominent parts of the local economy. As in literature, it is remarkable how many of the most familiar names in their fields had a local connection: the Rennies and the Brunels in engineering; Peek, Frean's for biscuits; Courage's and Barclay & Perkins for beer; and Crosse & Blackwell for processed foods. No local history of Southwark and Bermondsey could afford to neglect industry and commerce, given this background (and the traditional criticism of local history that it concerned itself with 'church and manor' and little else). This book seeks to give proper notice, especially in the second and third sections, to such major businesses as Hay's Wharf and Butler's Wharf, and to selected firms involved in engineering, food-processing and leather tanning. Many pictures throughout the book give incidental attention to the enormous number and variety of local businesses earlier this century.

Most of the photographs date from between about 1880 and the Second World War, when the traditional industries still flourished and when the local population was at its peak. Postwar changes have seen the old economy almost completely disappear, and with it many streets, buildings and institutions which these photographs serve to recall. The Leathersellers' Technical College, for example, was entirely appropriate in Bermondsey before the war (page 28); now it would be quite out of place. Perseverance Street, depicted on page 47, was typical of countless prewar streets in Bermondsey, but is now a vanished type.

Since 1965 all the areas in this book have been parts of the London Borough of Southwark. Between 1900 and 1965 they were divided into the Metropolitan Boroughs of Southwark and Bermondsey. This older Southwark included the former civil parish of St Mary Newington, which encompassed the Elephant and Castle and Walworth to the south of it. The Elephant and Castle is given a chapter to itself, as it is South London's best-known junction, gathering the routes from half a dozen Thames bridges because of the bend of the river between the Pool of London and Lambeth. The first bridge additional to London Bridge, which was the Westminster Bridge of 1750, led to the building of New Kent Road between the Old Kent Road and the old centre of Newington. It was no coincidence that a new public house called the Elephant and Castle appeared shortly afterwards at Newington as the traffic burgeoned. The photographs in that section reflect the vibrancy of the junction in the late nineteenth and early twentieth centuries, especially as a place for shopping – all the approach roads were lined with shops as well as the junction proper – before wartime bombing and postwar planning destroyed its established character.

Another major junction which has been ruined by postwar planning is the Bricklayers' Arms, where the Old Kent Road and New Kent Road meet. The flyover which was built there at the end of the 1960s removed so many historic landmarks that the junction is now a featureless waste which pedestrians avoid. What a different story the pictures in this book tell! The Old Kent Road itself lost its old renown for shops after the war, although in recent years it has partly regained its role through supermarkets with large car parks. The illustrations in this book show the area in its heyday, before traffic had overwhelmed it.

The Metropolitan Borough of Bermondsey incorporated the formerly separate district of Rotherhithe in 1900. Rotherhithe was quite distinct in its economy, for its life was dominated by ships and the sea. The nautical flavour of much of Rotherhithe's life was pronounced until after the Second World War. It had a significant shipbuilding industry down to the nineteenth century, and retained the industries of ship-repairing, and barge-building and barge-repairing, well into this century. The district included the only system of enclosed wet docks south of the Thames: the Surrey Commercial Docks, which specialized in timber and foodstuffs. In Rotherhithe's closing years as a separate local authority, in the 1890s, a substantial and ornate town hall was built in Lower Road, which this book illustrates in some detail for the first time.

Due attention is given in sections 13 and 14 to the Volunteers of Victorian and Edwardian times, and to their successors, the Territorials. Both Southwark and Bermondsey had their own volunteer regiment, which proudly paraded at so many civic events in the 1890s and early 1900s, and fought in the Boer War and in the two world wars. The regiment which was based in Southwark produced a winner of the Victoria Cross in the First World War (page 113) and contributed the band which led the victorious 47th (London) Division into Lille in northern France at the close of the First World War (page 114).

The book presents a balanced view of its districts in a relatively recent era, many parts of which people still remember, but which is increasingly remote in economic and social terms and even in respect of the layout of streets and the buildings which once stood in them. Here we have a precise record in pictures of that past world.

THE OLD TOWN OF SOUTHWARK

The ancient church of St Saviour, Southwark, was raised to the dignity of a cathedral in 1905. In the years before the First World War, it was furnished worthily in accordance with its new status. The eminent Gothic Revival architect George Frederick Bodley (1827–1907) designed the bishop's chair in this photograph almost at the end of his career. It was made of English oak and its back was decorated with linenfold panelling, the arms of the diocese and the words pax vobiscum (peace be with you). Bodley also designed the font of Verde di Prato marble at the west end of the nave. The architecture of the choir which can be seen here dates from the thirteenth century.

For many years before St Saviour's became a cathedral in 1905, it was prepared for the event. The nave which Henry Rose had designed in the 1830s was replaced in 1890–7 by Sir Arthur Blomfield. His architecture was always stately and competent, and here he based his work on the surviving thirteenth-century choir, thereby pulling the cathedral together through a uniformity of style. Blomfield's worthy contribution was greatly preferable to the fabric it replaced. In the 1890s and early 1900s a heartening number of benefactors came forward to give furnishings and embellishments to the church, and of those donors Sir Frederick Wigan, the head of the most prominent local firm of hop factors, was the doyen.

Borough High Street, next to St Saviour's Church (Southwark Cathedral), *c.* 1890. The approach to London Bridge seen here dated from 1831 when John Rennie's bridge was opened. The new approach seemed likely to threaten the church's Lady chapel, but the familiar four-gabled structure was kept and restored. The railway viaduct was brought into use in 1864 to take trains from Kent and the Channel ports to Charing Cross. The dome in the background was designed by Henry Rose for the Borough Market.

Cardinal's Wharf, 49 Bankside, *c.* 1935. This agreeable early Georgian house has been the subject of more myth-making than any other property in Southwark. It was NOT connected with Sir Christopher Wren or Catherine of Aragon, nor any notable in history; it was simply a typical house of its time which saw service chiefly as the property of coal merchants. It stands out because almost all its contemporaries in Bankside have gone. All the myths seem to have originated with the occupier, Malcolm Munthe, just after the Second World War. The passage to the right of the house is Cardinal Cap Alley.

Nancy's Steps, London Bridge, *c.* 1960. The steps on the upstream side of the Southwark approach to London Bridge provided the setting for the momentous meeting in Dickens's *Oliver Twist* between Mr Brownlow and Rose Maylie on the one hand, and Nancy herself on the other. Unfortunately for her, Nancy's warning to her visitors of Oliver's danger was overheard by the concealed Noah Claypole, whose subsequent report to Fagin led to Nancy's murder at the hands of Bill Sikes.

Memorial portrait of James Braidwood, 1861. The Superintendent of the Metropolitan Fire Engine Establishment, he was killed in the Great Fire of Tooley Street in 1861, when a wall fell on him. The fire engulfed many warehouses on the riverfront just downstream of London Bridge, in the vicinity of Hay's Dock, and was considered to be the worst fire in London since 1666. James Braidwood's funeral procession to Abney Park Cemetery at Stoke Newington was one of the largest London had ever seen.

A crowd assembles under the plaque commemorating the Globe Theatre, in Park Street, 1923. In the presence of the Mayor of Southwark, Canon T.P. Stevens of Southwark Cathedral is giving a lecture as part of the Shakespeare Commemoration in that year. William Shakespeare was owner of one-tenth of the Globe, which stood on this site from 1599 to 1644 (being rebuilt after a fire in 1613). His brother, Edmund, an actor, lived just off this street and when he died in 1607 he was buried at St Saviour's nearby.

Edward Edwards's Almshouses in Burrell Street, off Blackfriars Road, photographed by A.E. Wade, *c.* 1900. The foundation dates back to a deed of 1717. Land was bought in 1752 and the first almshouses were ready in 1753. A rebuilding took place in 1895 and another has occurred since.

The former Surrey Chapel, Blackfriars Road, *c.* 1890. The octagonal chapel was built for Rowland Hill in 1782–3, and he remained there as its minister until his death in 1833. His successor in 1876 migrated to a huge, new Gothic church opposite Lambeth North station. The old chapel was occupied by Methodists for five years and was then turned over to commercial use. It was destroyed in the Second World War. Its shape was an eighteenth-century fashion, probably derived from the Octagon Chapel in Norwich.

The beating of the bounds of Christ Church parish, Blackfriars Road, 1898. The photograph was taken at the workhouse in Marlborough Street. It was traditional in many parishes for a procession to be formed on Ascension Day to tour the parochial boundaries. A group of schoolboys would always be included in the procession, and long sticks were usually carried. Attention was paid in particular to inspecting boundary stones and plaques, such as the one in front of this group. Third from the right in the middle row is the Rector, A.H. De Fontaine; fourth from the right is R.W. Bowers, parochial historian of Christ Church.

The Bishop of Rochester, E.S. Talbot, speaking at the opening of the churchyard of Christ Church, Blackfriars Road, as a public garden, 16 June 1900. After closure, burial grounds in central London were often turned into public gardens in late Victorian times. In this case, the churchyard was laid out by the Metropolitan Public Gardens Association and was due to be maintained by the St Saviour's District Board of Works. Southwark Borough Council took it over at the end of 1900.

The Obelisk in St George's Circus, *c.* 1905. The opening of the first Blackfriars Bridge in 1769 and the laying out of Blackfriars Road (originally Great Surrey Street) led to the creation of St George's Circus in the former open land of St George's Fields. Robert Mylne designed the Obelisk, which was placed in the centre of the circus in 1771. Ninety years ago it was removed to the grounds of the Bethlem Royal Hospital (now the Imperial War Museum), but plans have been made to restore it to its original site.

King's Court Chapel, off Great Suffolk Street, *c*. 1900. This weatherboarded building had become a chapel on 11 April 1800, and originally housed a congregation of General Baptists who had previously worshipped in Duke Street nearby. By the late nineteenth century the building was run as a mission station of the Surrey Chapel in Blackfriars Road. It was closed because of disrepair in October 1901, and was demolished in about 1908.

Zoar Street in the 1930s. The population of old Southwark was once vastly greater than it is today, and before the Second World War there were many poor houses of the type seen here tucked away in alleys and narrow streets. Such properties have all but disappeared in the past half-century.

Collier's Rents, *c*. 1930. This narrow street connected Long Lane with the alley called Angel Place, which led into the Borough High Street. After the Second World War it was widened and re-aligned, and became Tennis Street. The building with the pediment was a former Congregational Chapel which had been built in about 1766. The low wall next to its façade bounded the chapel's small burial ground. All these buildings were destroyed in the Second World War.

Houses in St Thomas's Street, next to Guy's Hospital, 1914. These ornate façades are strongly reminiscent of the commercial buildings put up in Southwark Street in the 1860s and 1870s, with arched windows and Italianate detail. They were designed for the medical staff of Guy's by the local architects, Messrs Newman and Billing, in 1862, and stand out amid the Georgian reticence of St Thomas's Street.

TOOLEY STREET & THE WHARVES

Mr Alderman Humphery's dock and warehouses, 1857. John Humphery was the proprietor of Hay's Wharf, Southwark, between 1838 and 1863, in succession to Francis Theodore Hay, who was the last of the Hays to be involved in the business. John Humphery was an Alderman of the City of London and served as Lord Mayor in 1842–3; he was also the Member of Parliament for Southwark from 1832 to 1852. The warehouses he had built in Tooley Street by William Cubitt were the centrepiece of the biggest business in cargo-handling in Southwark.

Tea chests at Hay's Wharf, *c.* 1920. Until the early nineteenth century the wharf depended on coastal and short-sea trade but Alderman Humphery and his partners changed to a policy of worldwide trade. One of the partners, Arthur Magniac, was the son of a founder of the great oriental trading company of Jardine, Matheson. As a result, tea from China became an important commodity at Hay's Wharf. In the 1860s the famous tea clippers would race to the wharf from the other side of the world with the new season's tea. Indian tea entered the field later.

An inspector examining tinned food at Tower Bridge Wharf, 1957. This photograph was taken for Bermondsey Borough Council's Public Health Department.

Horse-drawn wagons in Battlebridge Lane in the heart of the Hay's Wharf empire, *c.* 1920. This photograph gives a good idea of the vast size of the warehouses and the scale of the business, given that it extended from Tower Bridge to upstream of London Bridge. These buildings are now part of 'London Bridge City'.

Courage's Brewery next to Tower Bridge, 1976. John Courage established his business here in 1787, more than a century before Tower Bridge was opened. In the eighteenth and nineteenth centuries there were many breweries along the south bank of the Thames; this one achieved greater fame than the rest. It was closed in 1981.

St Olave's Church in Tooley Street, *c.* 1925. A church had stood on the site since the eleventh century; its patron was the first Christian King of Norway, whose death in 1030 was reckoned to be a martyrdom. The church was last rebuilt to the designs of Henry Flitcroft in 1737–40, and it is his church we see here. By the early twentieth century the congregation had all but disappeared, for most of the parish was taken up by wharves. The church was closed in 1918; demolition followed for the body of the church in 1926 and for the tower in 1928.

The demolition of the body of St Olave's Church in 1926. Some of the fittings were removed to the new church of St Olave at Mitcham. The site in Tooley Street was used to build a new head office for Hay's Wharf.

St Olave's and St Saviour's Grammar School in Tooley Street, 1930. The Elizabethan school foundations of Southwark's two leading parishes had merged in 1896 and were housed in the building we see here, which was built in 1892–5 to the designs of the E.W. Mountford. The school moved to Orpington in Kent in 1968. The building in Tooley Street survives but is presently empty.

Staff of St Olave's and St Saviour's Grammar School, 1936. Henry George Abel, the headmaster from 1922 to 1937, is in the middle of the front row.

The Tower Bridge Hotel, *c.* 1910. This large and dignified building more or less formed a pair with a bank on the opposite corner, forming a 'gateway' to the Tower Bridge approach from Tooley Street.

Members of the St Olave's Brigade of the Oxford and Bermondsey Club, 1914. These working-class lads are dressed à la West End, down to such accessories as watch-chains and walking sticks. The East End aped the West End when smartness was the order of the day.

St Olave's Library, Tooley Street, 1933. The library had been opened in 1902 by the Metropolitan Borough of Bermondsey, for Tooley Street had passed into that authority's hands in 1900. The library stood next to the additional churchyard provided for St Olave's Parish in 1586 (left). In times past, this spot was the beginning of Horselydown, an open space on the eastern edge of the town of Southwark. The library was closed in 1970.

Shad Thames, 1971. This is a view worthy of a Piranesi of industrial Southwark, with wharves on both sides of the road connected at various heights by metal bridges. Most of this property belonged to Butler's Wharf, a very large business which dominated the waterfront between Tower Bridge and St Saviour's Dock, just as Hay's Wharf was supreme upstream of the bridge.

St Saviour's Dock at low tide, 1930. This small inlet of the Thames separated historic Southwark from historic Bermondsey, and was named after the great Cluniac monastery in Bermondsey. The original Peek, Frean's biscuit factory fronted the eastern side of this dock (on the right).

INDUSTRY & COMMERCE

Bankside, 1971. The warehouses which had lined the riverfront for so long were closing for good at this time, and the familiar riverside cranes were subsequently removed. Bankside was an industrial street a generation ago; now it is an office quarter and a haunt of tourists.

Grey & Marten Ltd's City Lead Works of 1880, Southwark Bridge Road, 1977. At one time lead works were numerous along the riverfront between Lambeth and Rotherhithe; lead shot towers appear in many old prints. These premises, which had a tall chimney (on the right), stood next to Southwark Bridge on its eastern or downstream side. The site is now occupied by the offices of the *Financial Times* and therefore serves to illustrate Southwark's postwar change from being an industrial quarter to being a district of offices.

The interior of Dewrance & Co. Ltd's factory in Great Dover Street in the 1930s. This was one of many large engineering works in Southwark and Bermondsey. The firm took its name from John Dewrance (1803–61), who was Locomotive Superintendent of the Liverpool & Manchester Railway. He was the nephew of the previous owner of the works in Great Dover Street, which dated back to about 1832. Dewrance's manufactured parts for railways, ships and power stations.

Stevenson & Howell Ltd ran a large factory in Great Suffolk Street and Bear Lane, Southwark, which was known as the Standard Works. There the firm distilled essences and essential oils. In this view, ginger mixers and percolators may be seen. The firm existed between 1882 and 1973, and the Southwark factory was opened in 1886. The photograph was taken soon after its closure.

The Leather Exchange in Leathermarket Street (left) and Weston Street (right), *c.* 1925. Bermondsey had boasted a thriving leather industry for centuries before the exchange was built in 1878 to a design by George Elkington & Sons. Above the ground-floor windows there were roundels with excellent carvings of leather manufacturing scenes. Note also the heavy porch supported by two Atlas figures. To the right is the Leather Market of 1833, a more subdued building whose only architectural pretensions are the giant pilasters visible under the words 'Trostel Leather Company'.

The Leathersellers' Company's Technical College, Tower Bridge Road, *c.* 1928. It had been opened in 1909 by the Worshipful Company of Leathersellers of the City of London to further the leather industry of the area. In 1951 it became the National College for the Leather Industry.

A mantelpiece in a ground-floor room of 148 Long Lane, photographed by R.J. Angel, Bermondsey's Borough Engineer and Surveyor, *c*. 1920. The carvings illustrate processes in leather manufacturing, including (in the centre) men holding long poles to move skins in and out of tanning pits. The mantelpiece was taken to the Guildhall Museum (now part of the Museum of London) in 1968.

Polishing skins at the Neckinger Leather Mills of Bevingtons & Sons, 1931. This firm was the most prominent in Bermondsey's leather manufacturing industry and had its main premises on each side of the railway viaduct in Abbey Street.

Just as Bermondsey had a leather exchange, so Southwark had a hop exchange to act as a focus for its characteristic trade. The building was designed by R.H. Moore and was constructed in 1866–7. It is seen here after a fire had badly damaged it in 1920. The two upper floors were afterwards removed, and the building was turned into offices called Central Buildings. In recent years its name has reverted to the Hop Exchange and it has undergone a creditable restoration. The great hall inside – the exchange floor – is Southwark's least-known important Victorian interior. A few years ago it was threatened by the railway's Thameslink scheme, but the threat appears to have gone. If any building in that vicinity deserves to be kept intact, it is the Hop Exchange.

Calvert's Buildings, 15 Southwark Street, during the Second World War. This building belonged to Wigan, Richardson & Co., the prominent firm of hop factors, and was one of the original industrial and commercial buildings which lined Southwark Street in the later nineteenth century. Sir Frederick Wigan, the head of the firm, was Southwark Cathedral's leading benefactor at the turn of this century. When the property was demolished, archaeologists found remains of substantial Roman buildings on the site. The name of the property derives from Felix Calvert, an eighteenth-century brewer, and was confusingly used of several buildings and an alley between Southwark Street and Borough High Street.

The King's Head Inn, Borough High Street, photographed by Henry Dixon in 1881. Many of Southwark's coaching inns were photographed at that time, for they were generally in the last stages of decline and threatened with demolition. This one was demolished in 1885. The yard survived, and a new public house was built in it. Henry Dixon took his pictures for the Society for Photographing Relics of Old London.

Spa Road station, Bermondsey, c. 1910. The London & Greenwich Railway was first opened from Spa Road to Deptford, and this station was the first London railway terminus. London Bridge station was opened a few months later in 1836. Spa Road station was closed in 1915. London's first railway was a huge commercial undertaking in the Southwark of the 1830s.

The 'halfpenny bumper', 1913. This was the name given to a one-horse tram which was run by the London County Council as route no. 90 between the Canal Bridge in the Old Kent Road to Raymouth Road. The view here is of St James's Road at its junction with Old Kent Road. The route was discontinued in July 1913. Another route, no. 88, ran between Rotherhithe and Tower Bridge Road until April 1915.

BERMONDSEY FOLK

A group outside the Bermondsey Settlement, Farncombe Street, c. 1905. One of the many repercussions of the Entente Cordiale of 1904 was that many French delegations visited South London at that time. The Bermondsey Settlement was the Methodist Church's social and educational mission to Bermondsey, founded in 1891 and run by Dr John Scott Lidgett for no fewer than fifty-eight years. Alfred Salter, the local GP and reforming politician, who had lived at the settlement before his marriage, is second from the left of the woman in white.

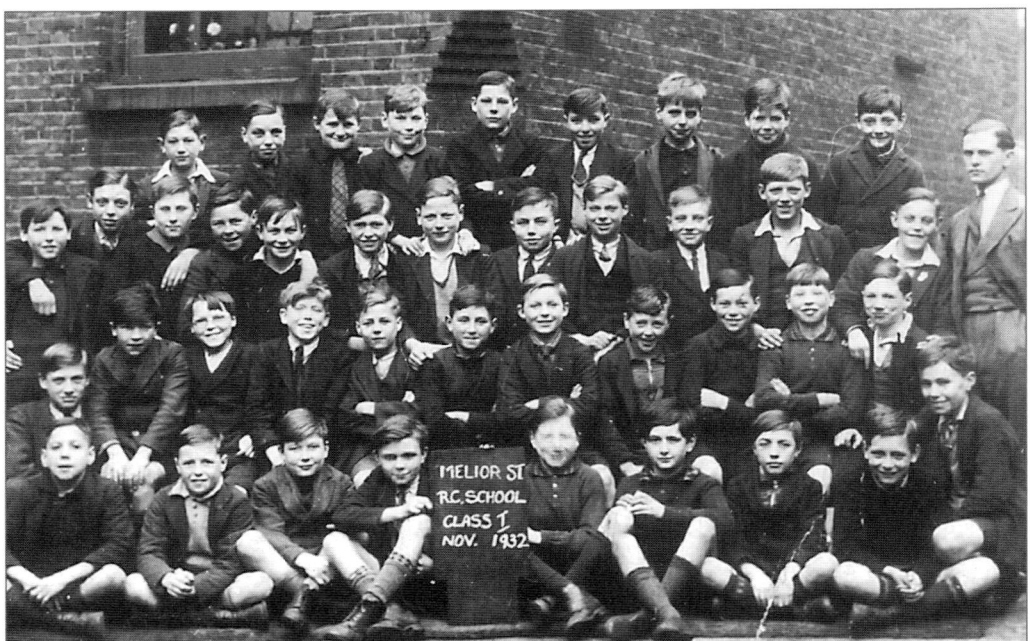

Class I of the Melior Street Roman Catholic School, November 1932. The church in Melior Street (Our Lady of La Salette and St Joseph) dates from 1861 and succeeded an earlier church in Webb Street which had been opened in 1848.

The choir at Laxon School, 1956. This late Victorian school was founded by the London School Board off Long Lane (between Crosby Row and Kipling Street), which has been swept away along with Laxon Street (from which it took its name), and most of the nineteenth-century houses which it once served.

The opening of the joy slide in St James's churchyard, 1921. It was donated by Arthur Carr, Chairman of Peek, Frean and Co. Ltd, and was made by W.J. Dixon & Son of Blue Anchor Lane. Arthur Carr stands in the middle, under the child with the outstretched arm. Somewhat improbably, this dignified captain of industry tried out the slide himself at the opening.

A children's slide in Long Lane Recreation Ground, September 1934.

The Labour Party at prayer. This is the West Bermondsey Labour Party at a service in St James's Church in 1931; Canon Donaldson is in the pulpit. The party's MP, Alfred Salter (who was a Quaker by his own choice), sits in the front row, third from the left of the banner.

Canon Edward Francis Murnane (1854–1933), 1926. He was the long-serving parish priest of Most Holy Trinity Church, the Roman Catholic church at Dockhead, and became one of Bermondsey's best-loved public figures. His funeral in 1933 was one of the biggest public events in Bermondsey between the wars. He left just £13 when he died.

The temperance movement arranged events in Southwark Park, and here in 1937 two local Labour MPs, Alfred Salter (left) and Charles George Ammon (right), are honouring the memory of a local nineteenth-century temperance pioneer, Jabez West. A fountain was placed in the park as a memorial to him.

Mrs Emily Blanche Carr-Gomm lays the foundation stone of the South Bermondsey Club and Institute on 25 January 1890. She was the niece of Field-Marshal Sir William Maynard Gomm and inherited the Manor of Rotherhithe from his widow in 1877.

Breakfast for local schoolchildren at Bermondsey Central Hall, 1934. Between 300 and 400 children were given cocoa, and bread with jam or dripping, without charge. The Central Hall, which had been opened in 1900, was the principal Methodist church in Bermondsey.

The Mayor of Bermondsey, Miss Eileen Greenwood, and members of the Bermondsey Veterans' Club examine parcels sent from the Alexander Miller Memorial Homes, Geelong West, Victoria, Australia, on 9 November 1950. The old folk in the Australian town had saved up to send gifts to their Bermondsey contemporaries, who still faced rationing at the time.

Harold Glanville, the Liberal victor in Bermondsey in the general election of January 1910. He won back the seat for the Government party which John Dumphreys had seized for the Conservatives at a by-election in 1909 (*see* page 53).

Some workmen of the Bermondsey Borough Council in Rotherhithe Street in the late 1920s.

The opening ceremony of the Bermondsey Flower Show, 1927. This is the gallery of the Town Hall in Spa Road.

Bermondsey Labour Fair at the Central Baths in Grange Road, December 1927.

BERMONDSEY LANDMARKS

The toll house in Jamaica Road, which was closed on 30 November 1865. Toll houses and toll gates were once numerous in London's streets. Names such as Camberwell Gate and New Cross Gate still recall them.

Parker's Row, 1907. The premises of Alfred Parker, a vehicle builder, stood in front of Most Holy Trinity Church, a Roman Catholic church built in 1834–5. On the other side of the church was the convent of the Sisters of Mercy, which A.W.N. Pugin, the famous Gothic Revival architect, had designed. This area was very badly bombed in the Second World War, and both church and convent had to be rebuilt. The present church is a distinguished building by H.S. Goodhart-Rendel and was opened in 1960. At the time of this photograph, the main route from London Bridge towards Rotherhithe went via Dockhead, Parker's Row and the present Old Jamaica Road, making a large reversed S on the map. In the early 1960s the topography of the area was altered quite considerably. The present Jamaica Road cuts across the area in a straight line from the end of Tooley Street, and Parker's Row is now a backwater.

The interior of Christ Church, Parker's Row, *c.* 1923. This church stood at the southern end of Parker's Row, at the junction with George Row. It had been built in 1848 to the neo-Norman designs of W. Bennett Hayes; it was fashionable to build in a Norman style in the 1840s. Christ Church was one of the numerous nineteenth-century churches to be built in the ancient parish of Bermondsey, as the population grew rapidly and the Church of England sought to maintain an influence. Its construction was helped by the Southwark Fund for Schools and Churches, which was a typical Victorian scheme for church-building in a poor district. In the twentieth century, by contrast, the Church has been in retreat. Christ Church was demolished in 1967.

A group outside the front door of Bermondsey Workhouse, Tanner Street, almost certainly at the time of King George V's coronation in 1911. This had originally been the workhouse of Bermondsey parish and had passed into the hands of the St Olave's Board of Guardians (later the Bermondsey Board of Guardians) in the later nineteenth century. In 1911 it was almost at the end of its existence. During the First World War part of it became the King Albert Hospital for Belgian Soldiers. Subsequently the buildings were demolished and a recreation ground was laid out on the site. The top of the tower from St Olave's Church in Tooley Street was set up in the recreation ground after the tower's demolition in 1928.

The premises of T. Layman Ltd at 171–177 Jamaica Road, *c*. 1930. Layman's was a pawnbroker's and sold various secondhand goods. The street on the left is Martin Street and the viewpoint is roughly from the junction of Jamaica Road and Major Road. Showing above the roofline are the two turrets of Jamaica Row Chapel, which was the oldest Free Church foundation in the area. It originated in the seventeenth century, and after surviving persecution in the days of King Charles II, it settled down to being a leading non-Anglican 'cause'. The Victorian building in this photograph was destroyed in the Second World War.

This is the view looking north behind the backs of houses in Kipling Street (right) and Lockyer Street (left), towards St Paul's Church, *c.* 1935. The church dated from 1848 and was designed by S.S. Teulon, who was also responsible for the nearby St Stephen's in Manciple Street. It was demolished in 1963, in a period when Bermondsey's nineteenth-century ecclesiastical inheritance was rapidly been cast away. Kipling Street was known as Nelson Street until 1892; this renaming came remarkably early in Rudyard Kipling's career. At top right can be seen the ventilation tower at Hunt's House in Guy's Hospital; in many views of Southwark, it appeared to be another church spire.

Perseverance Street, January 1936. This decidedly dreary street ran from Druid Street to Neckinger Street near Dockhead. Many Bermondsey streets looked like this until the Blitz and must have needed the virtue of perseverance to be tolerable.

The north-west corner of Thorburn Square, 1963. The demolition of this square of mid-Victorian houses, facing St Anne's Church in the centre, was a great pity.

Bridge House, George Row, 1937. This property, whose most familiar feature was the shell hood over the doorway, dated from about 1700 and was a survivor from the days when well-to-do merchants lived near the Bermondsey waterfront. Until the mid-nineteenth century, the proprietors of many Bermondsey businesses lived on the spot. Bridge House, after surviving the huge changes in the area in the Victorian era and escaping the Blitz, fell to redevelopment in 1958.

Bermondsey Square, *c.* 1900. The square was originally the courtyard of Bermondsey Abbey, which was entered through a gateway from what is now Abbey Street. Before the laying-out of Tower Bridge Road in 1902, the two exits on its eastern side were Long Walk (to the north) and Grange Walk (to the south).

Southwark Park Road, with St Crispin's Church in the background, *c.* 1910. The church was destroyed in the Second World War but was rebuilt in 1958–9 by Thomas F. Ford. St Crispin was the patron saint of cordwainers or shoemakers, who took their name from the Spanish city of Cordova, a famous leather centre. In view of Bermondsey's large and ancient leather industry, St Crispin was an entirely appropriate patron for a local parish church.

Bermondsey Square, *c.* 1928. The road in the foreground is Tower Bridge Road, which sliced off the eastern side of Bermondsey Square in 1902. The petrol station stood where part of the New Caledonian Market is now held. The warehouse in the background fronted Abbey Street, opposite St Mary Magdalen's churchyard.

The Bermondsey Bookshop at 89 Bermondsey Street, June 1923. Sidney and Ethel Gutman founded the bookshop in 1921 'to bring books and the love of books into Bermondsey'. It was first housed at 89 Bermondsey Street and later at no. 171. It was more of a mission and a literary club than an ordinary bookshop, and many well-known writers of the time were invited to its meetings or to contribute to its journal, *The Bermondsey Book*. This curious episode of local literary history lasted until 1930.

MUNICIPAL BERMONDSEY

A Bermondsey street-washing vehicle outside a Council depot, August 1934. The Metropolitan Borough of Bermondsey existed from 1900 to 1965. Its incorporation in a larger borough in 1965 was unpopular and the memory of the old corporation still manages to arouse expressions of affection and loyalty today.

Colonel Samuel Bourne Bevington (1832–1907), the first Mayor of Bermondsey (in 1900–2). He was the head of the leather firm of Bevingtons & Sons, the largest local firm in the trade, whose principal premises were the Neckinger Leather Mills in Abbey Street. He took a leading part in the Volunteer movement in Victorian times, and for a long time commanded the 3rd Volunteer Battalion, The Queen's (Royal West Surrey Regiment). For the Volunteers he built a drill hall next to the leather mills, on the corner of Old Jamaica Road (*see* page 116). He was eventually accorded a full-length statue in Tooley Street: a very rare honour for a local politician.

John Molesworth Thomas Dumphreys, Mayor of Bermondsey, *c.* 1906. He was one of Edwardian Bermondsey's best-known politicians, with his white side-whiskers and his distinctive viewpoint as 'a Conservative working man'. He was a leather shaver who became an ardent tariff reformer, standing in that cause against Joseph Chamberlain in Birmingham in 1885; ironically, because Chamberlain later became the leading proponent of tariff reform and defected from the Liberals to the Conservatives. In 1909 Dumphreys won a by-election as a Conservative for the Bermondsey seat, only to lose it at the general election of January 1910. He served as an alderman on Bermondsey Borough Council and was elected Mayor for the municipal year, 1906–7. He died in 1925.

The laying of the foundation stone of the municipal offices in Spa Road, October 1928. The handsome Greek Classical building which resulted still stands at the corner of Spa Road and Neckinger. H. Tansley was its designer. After the Second World War it became Bermondsey's Town Hall. In this photograph, Alfred Salter, MP for Bermondsey, stands on the right.

The Mayor of Bermondsey, William Bustin, and his wife at the laying of the foundation stone of the Silver Walk Estate, Rotherhithe, 1922. Municipal housing in Bermondsey and Rotherhithe was very limited until after the Labour Party won control of Bermondsey Borough Council in 1922; the scheme being started here was one of the few earlier ones. The Mayoress was widely known as Madame Annie Ryall, under which name she was a Gospel singer for many years. She and her husband ran the Bermondsey Gospel Mission at Dockhead.

Bermondsey Vestry Officers' dinner at the Bridge House Hotel, Southwark, 1898. The Vestry in the late nineteenth century was run on very similar lines to the Borough Council of the early twentieth century. The venue for this dinner was at the foot of London Bridge and had been the first railway hotel in London in the 1830s.

Alexandra Rose Day, 1935. The Mayor of Bermondsey, Councillor Sidney Weightman, is pictured on the steps of Bermondsey Town Hall, Spa Road, with collectors and supporters. The annual summer collection was named after Queen Alexandra (1844–1925), the wife of King Edward VII, and was for the benefit of hospital patients.

The last parade of Bermondsey Borough Council's horses in May 1953; they were subsequently discharged from Council service. One horse, a nine-year-old called Mickey, was given to Brookfield Naval Training School at Newport on the Isle of Wight, where it was reported that he missed the crowded London streets. The boys of the school then groomed him for entry in the Royal Isle of Wight Agricultural Show, at which he won the third prize: a very honourable retirement for a Bermondsey dustcart horse.

Staff of Bermondsey Borough Council's Electricity Department, 1947. Before the nationalization of the industry in 1948, electricity in many districts was supplied by municipal undertakings.

Bermondsey Borough Council's engineers' shop, 1937. This was part of the Neckinger Depot, where repairs were carried out to vehicles and other Council property.

Children at Bermondsey Central Library in Spa Road, 1925. The early public libraries in London tended to be formal and rather earnest places. Between the wars there were attempts to make them more open and attractive to the public, and this involved some attention to children's interests.

Staff of Bermondsey Public Libraries, 1929. The Chief Librarian of the day, James D. Stewart, sits in the middle of the front row. He was in office from 1923 to 1950. To the left of him is Leonard Hobbs, who ran Rotherhithe Library and wrote about Rotherhithe's history in the local press. The Chief Librarian from 1950 to 1965, Percy Clare, stands at the far right of the top row.

The presentation of Volume II of *Defensiones Theologiae Thomae Aquinatis* by Bermondsey Central Library to the Henry E. Huntingdon Library, San Marino, California, 23 July 1951. The book was written by Johannes Capreolus, a fifteenth-century French theologian, and was printed in Venice in 1483. Bermondsey Libraries owned one volume of a four-volume set, and the Huntingdon Library owned the remaining three. The resulting set was the only one in the United States of America in 1951. The donation is made here by R.H. Hadow, British Consul-General (seventh from right), to Dr Robert A. Millikan, Chairman of the library's board of trustees (sixth from right). The seventh person from the left is the world-famous astronomer Edwin P. Hubble, whose study of distant galaxies showed that the universe is expanding. He was a trustee of the Huntingdon Library.

A delivery of books to a reader's home, 1959. A service to the aged and infirm in their own homes has long been part of public library provision in the London boroughs. The librarian is Charles Wilson.

Bermondsey Borough Council's mobile library at the Amos Estate, Rotherhithe, May 1961. The mobile library had come into operation in 1960. It was 26 ft long and could carry 2,000 books.

The living room of a new flat on the Vauban Estate, 1934. This estate, off Spa Road, was built by Bermondsey Borough Council in 1932–4 and comprised 124 flats and seven shops. It was one of a large number of new interwar estates with which the council replaced Georgian and Victorian houses.

The bedroom of a new flat on the Vauban Estate, 1934.

ROTHERHITHE SCENES

Boating on the lake in Southwark Park, just before the First World War. The lake had been laid out in 1885 and had been much extended in 1908. It was a very popular feature of the park earlier this century.

Rotherhithe Town Hall, Lower Road, *c.* 1900. This substantial building was designed by Messrs Murray and Foster and was constructed in 1895–7. Although it was called a town hall, strictly speaking it was a vestry hall, as it was built for the Vestry of the Parish of St Mary, Rotherhithe. After Rotherhithe and Bermondsey merged in 1900, a town hall was not needed in Lower Road, and the building became a public library. It was destroyed by bombing in the Second World War. The main doorway was distinguished by the Greek female figures or caryatids which acted the part of flanking columns; they were sculpted by Henry Poole.

The chamber where Rotherhithe Vestry met, *c.* 1900. This was situated on the first floor of the Town Hall in Lower Road, at the front of the building. It was 50 ft long, 30 ft wide and 23 ft high. Over the doors leading into the chamber there was placed a panel to illustrate the industries of Rotherhithe. The Surrey Docks, shipbuilding and the timber trade were all represented. The designer was Miss E.M. Hope. In the centre was the Vestry's seal, showing two shipwrights supporting a shield bearing a ship.

The public hall at Rotherhithe Town Hall, *c.* 1900. This was placed at the back of the building and was as high as the two storeys at the front. It was entered from Moodkee Street and could seat 891 people.

Christ Church, Jamaica Road. This church was designed by Lewis Vulliamy and was built in 1838–9. It was one of three daughter-churches of St Mary's, Rotherhithe, which were founded in as many years under Edward Blick, Rector of Rotherhithe from 1835 to 1867. The church was closed in 1950 and was demolished in 1979. It appears in many photographs of Jamaica Road in the earlier twentieth century, for it had a prominent site on the corner of Cathay Street.

The Jolly Sailor, Lower Road, *c.* 1891. The building was demolished in that year and its replacement lasted until 1945. A public house had stood on this site when Lower Road ran between fields.

Cathay Street, looking towards the Angel public house, February 1937. This road had been called Love Lane until 1892. To the right is the site of King Edward III's moated manor house which had been built in the middle of the fourteenth century; some of its foundations may be seen there today. The Angel is the earliest recorded public house in Rotherhithe.

Canon Edward Josselyn Beck, *c.* 1900. He served as Rector of Rotherhithe from 1867 to 1907 and left posterity in his debt by writing a history of the parish, entitled *Memorials to Serve for a History of the Parish of St Mary, Rotherhithe* (Cambridge University Press, 1907). He retired to Cambridge and died in 1923.

The sanctuary of St Mary's Church, 1926. The reredos or screen of honour for the altar was carved for the new church in the early eighteenth century by Joseph Wade, King's Carver in HM Dockyard at Deptford, whose memorial is still in the church. At one time the panels were inscribed with the Creed, the Ten Commandments and the Lord's Prayer rather than featuring the paintings seen here.

Prince Olav, then the Crown Prince of Norway, unveils a memorial at the opening of St Olave's Church for Norwegian seamen, June 1927. The memorial was given by Norwegian shipowners to commemorate the 2,101 Norwegian seamen killed in the First World War. This view is looking down what is now Jamaica Road; the tram on the left is in Lower Road. The public house on the right is the Princess Victoria.

St Olav's Church, *c.* 1930. This prominent landmark next to Rotherhithe Tunnel's entrance was built in 1926–7 in succession to the building in Redriff Road which is now the Docklands Settlement. Its presence recalls the Scandinavian sailors who brought cargoes of timber to the Surrey Commercial Docks.

Bryan's Court or Alley, *c.* 1935. The view looks towards Holy Trinity Church at the corner of Rotherhithe Street and Trinity Road (afterwards Bryan Road). The church dated from 1838–9 and was to be destroyed in the Second World War. A smaller building was erected on the site in 1959–60.

New council houses in Rotherhithe Street, 1930. They were built by Bermondsey Borough Council and were markedly attractive in contrast to the blocks of tenements which were being constructed almost everywhere at that time. Note the timber shed in the Surrey Commercial Docks in the background at the left and part of Redriff School on the right.

A Rotherhithe women's sporting group, *c.* 1895. Such a picture would be normal enough for a girls' college or public school, but it is a great rarity for an area such as Rotherhithe.

The entrance to Rotherhithe Tunnel, 1909. The tunnel had been built in 1904–8 by the London County Council to the designs of Maurice Fitzmaurice. The prominent gauge arch had been a cutting edge of a tunnelling shield.

May Day sports in Southwark Park, 1931.

Children from Classes 1 and 2 of Albion Primary School pictured at Sandown during a school trip to the Isle of Wight, 1961.

ROTHERHITHE
& THE THAMES

A view in the Surrey Commercial Docks, 1914. The characteristic gabled profile of timber sheds looms up in the background. Timber was Rotherhithe's staple trade until a generation ago.

The Thames at Rotherhithe, 1953. The spire of St Mary's Church is visible in the centre. To the right, the tall chimney of Gillman & Spencer's mill looms over the rather bare side wall of 41 Rotherhithe Street (*see* page 74). Just to the left of the crane, the Angel public house occupies its ancient site next to Rotherhithe Stairs. Note the large number of barges or lighters along the waterfront. Lighters ferried goods from the enclosed wet docks to the wharves (and vice versa), and many were built and repaired along this stretch of the river.

Barge renovation at the premises of Talbot Brothers Ltd, *c*. 1930. This was Norway Wharf, which lay immediately upstream of the South Metropolitan Gas Company's property. The jetty at which the gas company's colliers were unloaded can be seen in the background. Thomas Talbot founded the business, which his three sons continued. At one time the firm was the biggest builder of barges in Rotherhithe.

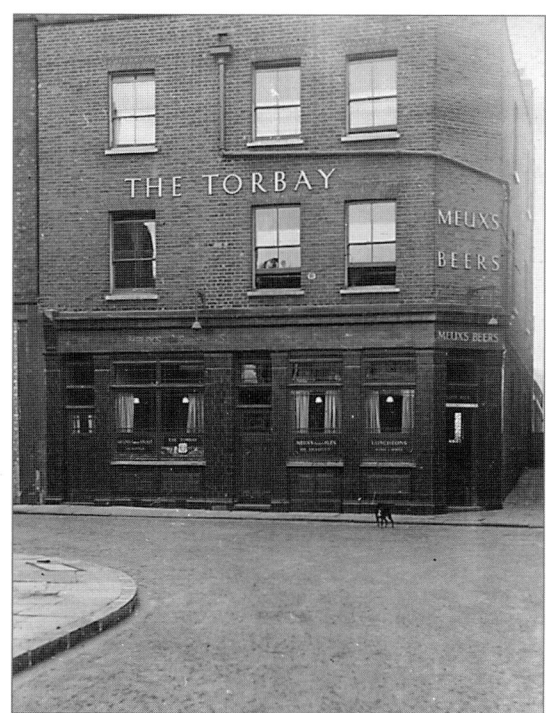

The Torbay, Rotherhithe Street, 1949. A public house of that name stood next to Elephant Stairs (right) from at least 1757 until 1955. The road in the foreground is Elephant Lane.

No. 41 Rotherhithe Street, 1976. The solitary house on the riverfront for long belonged to Braithwaite & Dean, lightermen. King's Stairs (*see* page 76) were immediately to the left of it. The Second World War destroyed the properties between no. 41 and the Angel; those to the right (downstream) were needlessly destroyed by the London County Council in the early 1960s.

River scene at Rotherhithe, 1914. The Lower Pool was markedly busy in those days with ocean-going steamers, colliers from the north-east and, above all, barges.

Ken Collins with the Mayor of Bermondsey, Councillor T. Hendy, in 1957, after he had won Doggett's Coat and Badge race. This race, founded by Thomas Doggett in 1715, traditionally promised great honour for young Thames watermen.

An aerial view of part of the Surrey Commercial Docks, 1926. The huge lines of timber sheds and vast spreads of floating timber can clearly be seen. Nelson Dock is prominent in the left foreground. At that time it was one of only two surviving yards at Rotherhithe for the repair of ships. It survived until 1968.

King's Stairs, 1911. River stairs were the traditional means of access to the Thames for the watermen, who ran the river's small passenger boats. There were as many as twenty public ways to the river at Rotherhithe. King's Stairs were next to 41 Rotherhithe Street (the middle building in this photograph). The name, and that of King Street (later Fulford Street), probably came from King Edward III's manor house nearby. Henry Pocock's on the left was a barge builder's; No. 41 was occupied by George Henry Leggett, a mast and oar maker; and to the right lay the Dover Castle public house.

THE ELEPHANT & CASTLE

The Elephant and Castle public house, rebuilt in 1898 by John Warren, dominates this view of about 1910.
Walworth Road ran to the left of it, Newington Butts to the right. A public house of this name had stood on
the site from at least 1765. On the right is the famous Rabbits' shoe shop and factory.

The southern end of Newington Causeway, ending with the Rockingham Arms public house on the corner of New Kent Road, 1858. To its left is Tarn & Co.'s shop, which later expanded to become the Elephant and Castle's largest business. On the right, the Elephant and Castle public house is shown across the junction on the corner of Newington Butts.

The corner of Newington Causeway (left) and New Kent Road (right), c. 1910. The building in the middle is the Rockingham Arms public house, which had been rebuilt in 1888. The façade to the left is part of the huge store of Isaac Walton & Co., which had superseded Tarn's. All the buildings here other than the public house had belonged to Tarn's. Note the no. 1 bus entering the junction: an early motor bus which originally terminated in New Kent Road.

The Elephant and Castle's huge cinema, the Trocadero, was opened in 1930 in New Kent Road on part of Tarn's old site. The developers were Philip and Sidney Hyams. It was famous for its substantial Wurlitzer organ, which was eventually re-erected in South Bank University by the Cinema Organ Society. The Trocadero was closed in 1963 and was demolished in the following year.

This view of about 1912 looks across the Elephant and Castle junction to the famous public house and to Newington Butts in the background on the right. The building of Freeman, Hardy & Willis had previously belonged to Rabbits', the shoemakers, established in 1846 and one of the best-known businesses in the area. On the left there is an entrance to the Elephant's first subway system, built in 1910–11.

The Metropolitan Tabernacle was built in 1859–61 to the designs of W.W. Pocock for the 'prince of preachers', Charles Haddon Spurgeon (1834–1892). He had become the minister of New Park Street Baptist Chapel, Southwark, in 1854, where his huge success as a preacher soon prompted a search for bigger premises and led to the building of Southwark's most capacious church, seen here in about 1890.

The Metropolitan Tabernacle could hold nearly 5,000 people when it was opened in 1861. The interior, shown here in about 1890, was arranged as in a theatre, focusing on the pulpit. The church was burnt in 1898 and was rebuilt on a slightly smaller scale. It was then bombed in 1941 and was again rebuilt by R. Mountford Pigott behind its familiar façade by 1959.

Palmer's had two shops at 39 and 48 London Road. The one shown here in 1904 stood opposite the South London Palace, a famous music hall, where one well-known performer, George Chirgwin, regularly ended his turn by saying, 'I must go over and have a basin full at Palmer's.'

W.A. Starr's shop in Newington Causeway, 14 February 1904. To its left can just be seen a part of the Alfred's Head public house, which faced the Elephant and Castle across the junction.

The staff of the St Mary Newington Schools, *c.* 1888. The girls' and boys' schools had moved to a site on the western side of Newington Butts in 1851, representing a foundation which was already a century and a half old. The schools stood next to the church of St Mary Newington, to whose parish they belonged.

Standards VI and VII at St Mary Newington Boys' School, April 1911. The desks seen here remained in many local schools until a generation after the Second World War.

THE OLD KENT ROAD & THE BRICKLAYERS' ARMS

The Old Kent Road has long been famous for its public houses. The World Turned Upside Down, seen here in about 1910, still exists next to the tenements shown on page 85, though it has since been rebuilt.

The Bricklayers' Arms junction seen from the New Kent Road, May 1963. This was a few years before the megalomaniac flyover scheme destroyed numerous historic buildings in the area and removed almost all its character. Among the casualties were the public house on the right in the background and Old Kent Road Library (left).

The Old Kent Road Library decorated for the coronation of King George VI, 1937. The library had been built in 1907–8 to the designs of Claude Batley and was the most architecturally distinguished library in Southwark. It stood at the junction of New Kent Road (left) and Old Kent Road (right) until it was destroyed to make way for the Bricklayers' Arms flyover in 1967.

Old Kent Road, *c.* 1950. The entrance to the Bricklayers' Arms railway goods' yard is on the left. This had opened as a passenger terminus in 1844. The big blocks of tenements behind the tram still stand today, whereas trams disappeared in 1952.

Just north of the Bricklayers' Arms junction there stood Hartley's jam factory, seen here in 1934. Its buildings remain, but the firm has gone. This is a view from the factory towards Bermondsey Central Hall, with Tower Bridge in the distance.

Union Crescent, New Kent Road, *c.* 1903. This modest but agreeable feature of Georgian Southwark is shown just before its demolition to make way for the St Saviour's and St Olave's Grammar School for Girls. The crescent, which was built for John Rolls I in 1783, faced and complemented the much grander Paragon (*see* page 87) across New Kent Road.

Staff of St Saviour's and St Olave's Grammar School for Girls, New Kent Road, 1927. The Headmistress, Miss M.G. Frodsham, is in the middle of the second row from the front. The school had been opened in 1903.

The Southwark Paragon was built in 1787–8 to the designs of Michael Searles on land belonging to the Rolls Estate. John Rolls II, the estate's owner in the early nineteenth century, reserved a house for himself from 1802 to 1804. The Paragon was one of Southwark's most important developments, both architecturally and socially, and it was incredible that it was largely demolished to provide a site for the Paragon School in 1898.

A girls' class at Paragon School, Searles Road, *c.* 1910. This school is described in Leonard J. Carter's book, *Walworth 1929–1939*. In the interwar years, the schoolkeeper was Joe Bent, who had won the VC in the First World War. During that war, a torpedo boat destroyer called HMS *Paragon* was 'adopted' by the school.

Paragon Gardens and Paragon School in the early twentieth century. This was the view which superseded that on page 87. The school was opened in 1900.

Nos 211–217 Old Kent Road, the headquarters of George Carter & Sons, tailors and hatters, 1973. At its centenary in 1951, this firm had twenty-five shops. The bowler hat on the figure above the clock was raised on the hour.

The church of St Mary Magdalene in Massinger Street, just off the Old Kent Road, became known as the pearlies' church. The priest seen here in the foreground was Alfred William Barker, Vicar of St Mary Magdalene's (1923–1938) and unofficial 'Bishop of the Old Kent Road'. He arranged an annual service and parade for the Pearly Kings and Queens and their families at harvest festival time. This photograph dates from 1938.

No. 32 Old Kent Road, the premises of Peter Kilpatrick, 1897. The Old Kent Road was one of Southwark's most important shopping streets, and the heyday of its shops ran from about 1880 to 1939. Previously, it had been a principal street of the costermongers. Kilpatrick's became the site of the Old Kent Road Library (*see* page 84).

WALWORTH SCENES

Clayton House, Manor Place, the premises of the Newington Reform Club, before 1894. Votes are sought for C.W. Norton, the Liberal candidate for Newington West, almost certainly in the general election of 1892, for Clayton House was demolished in 1894 and Norton was not a candidate for this seat until 1892. He served as the MP for Newington West from 1892 to 1916, when, despite his previous urging for the abolition of the House of Lords, he joined their lordships as the first Lord Rathcreedan. The site of Clayton House was taken by Newington Baths in 1898.

The Mayor of Southwark, Walter C. Williams, heads this group at a horse parade outside Manor Place Baths in 1912. This picture was taken from roughly the same spot as that on page 91. Southwark Borough Council (and its predecessor, the Vestry of St Mary Newington) ran a depot in Manor Place, which required the services of a great many horses. Parades were held regularly, and people took much pride in turning out well-groomed horses, and carts and harnesses in spotless condition.

Newington Vestry Hall on the corner of Walworth Road and Wansey Street, *c.* 1900. The Vestry of the Parish of St Mary Newington built this hall in 1864–5 to meet in and to accommodate the parochial administration. The site had belonged to the Fishmongers' Company of the City of London. Henry Jarvis, who designed the building, was a prolific local architect. In 1900, when the Vestry of St Mary Newington was superseded by Southwark Borough Council, this building became the Town Hall and was then enlarged. It remains in municipal ownership and use.

Surrey Square, 1964. Michael Searles designed this terrace, which was built in the early 1790s on land owned by the Driver family. In 1803 Edward Driver wrote: '. . . the architect is the true creator of a building and no one will deny that the concept of these noble façades was his and his alone'. The terrace was never part of a formal square as in Bloomsbury or Belgravia. One end of it was demolished to make way for a school at the beginning of this century. It is very fortunate that most of it survives, for Walworth has lost so much of its Georgian fabric.

Tenement blocks in Lion Street, off New Kent Road, 1966. Large parts of Walworth were once occupied by such late Victorian tenements, which were always referred to locally as 'the buildings'. These blocks were demolished in 1972 to make way for the Heygate Estate. In their last years, such tenements were roundly condemned as unbearable slums, yet when they were new, they were generally seen as improvements upon what they had replaced.

Henry Syer Cuming (1817–1902), 1897. At his death he left a large collection of papers and objects to the Metropolitan Borough of Southwark, which duly became the Cuming Museum above the library in the Walworth Road. The collection had been started by his father, Richard, as far back as 1782. The papers amassed by father and son speak eloquently of the comfortable lives of two amateur scholars in nineteenth-century Walworth. Henry lived at 63 Kennington Park Road in his later years. He served as Vice-President of the British Archaeological Association.

Houses in Kennington Park Road about to be demolished, 1913. They had been built in 1776 as Canterbury Row, for the Dean and Chapter of Canterbury had long owned the Manor of Walworth. The church in the background is St Mary Newington, built in 1876. These handsome Georgian houses were replaced by blocks of Guinness Buildings.

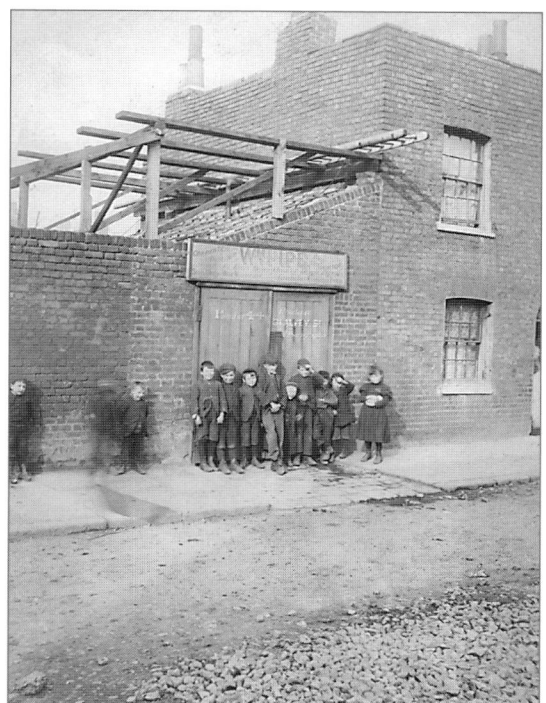

These children are standing outside the premises in Clandon Street where George Tinworth (1843–1913) had once helped his father, who was a wheelwright. Tinworth rose from these humble beginnings to become a noted sculptor in terracotta for Doulton & Co., the Lambeth potters.

Walworth Road station, in John Ruskin Street, had a narrow entrance which was called 'the shoot'. This cartoon of 1876 highlights the problem. The station closed for good in 1916 but there is still a Station Tavern next to the railway viaduct in John Ruskin Street.

A bust of Michael Faraday is unveiled by Lt-Col. Kenelm Edgcumbe, President of the Institution of Electrical Engineers, on 17 October 1928, in Southwark Central Library, Walworth Road. Faraday had been born in 1791 in Newington Butts and has been commemorated locally in several ways. The Mayor of Southwark (on the right) was Councillor W.F. Castle.

Staff celebrating the end of the Second World War at Southwark Central Library, 1945. The man sitting at the head of the left-hand table, Sidney Herbert Cox, lived to be 95, despite having been wounded in the First World War.

The milliner's shop of B. Wallach in Walworth Road, photographed between the wars. Note the large hanging lamps which were typical of early twentieth-century shopfronts.

The dining room at the Surrey Gardens in Manor Place, 1858. Between 1831 and 1878 the Surrey Gardens offered a wide range of public entertainment on the land which had belonged to Walworth's Manor House. Concerts, a zoo, firework displays and panoramas were among the attractions. The grounds were landscaped by Henry Phillips. In 1856 the Surrey Music Hall was built in the grounds to the designs of Horace Jones, and this photograph is of an interior of that building.

THE CHURCHES OF WALWORTH

The laying of the foundation stone of St Stephen's, Walworth Common (later Westmoreland Road), by Robert Stephen Faulconer, 1870. This was one of seventeen Anglican churches built in Walworth in the nineteenth century. St Stephen's was bombed in the Second World War and was not rebuilt.

Walworth Road Baptist Church, 1960. This substantial building could hold 1,000 people and was built in 1863–4 just a few hundred yards from Spurgeon's Metropolitan Tabernacle. Clearly, there was no shortage of churchgoers in Walworth in the 1860s. It was typical of the Baptists to build in the Classical style when other denominations had turned to Gothic. It was closed in 1969 and demolished in 1970.

The interior of Walworth Road Baptist Church at harvest festival time, probably early in the twentieth century. The pulpit and organ usually dominated the interiors of chapels belonging to the Baptists, Congregationalists and Methodists.

The Surrey Tabernacle, Wansey Street, 1960. This was yet another large Baptist church, built in 1864–5 for the noted Strict Baptist preacher, James Wells. It stood very close to Walworth Road Baptist Church. From 1927 to 1960 it served as the Borough Synagogue, in succession to the building shown below. The former Surrey Tabernacle was demolished in 1970.

The Borough Synagogue, Heygate Street, *c.* 1912. This building dated from 1867. The congregation consisted very largely of local shopkeepers. From 1927 its members used the old Surrey Tabernacle (above).

Crossway Congregational Church, New Kent Road, 1960. This substantial building was opened by the London Congregational Union in 1905 and lasted until 1972. It is typical of turn-of-the-century 'central halls', which were intended for vigorous evangelism in cities. A new Crossway Church was opened on the site in 1975.

St John's Church, Larcom Street, *c.* 1900. The building had been designed by Henry Jarvis in Early English style and was constructed in 1859–60. This is one of the South London churches which the Bishops of London consecrated in the mid-Victorian period, for only in that era did the Diocese of London ever extend south of the Thames.

The funeral of eight boy scouts at St John's Church, Larcom Street, 1912. The boys, who had belonged to the Dulwich Mission Troop attached to St John's, had drowned off Leysdown-on-Sea on the Isle of Sheppey on 4 August. The body of a ninth scout had not been found. The destroyer, HMS *Fervent*, had brought the bodies from Sheppey to Cherry Garden Pier in Bermondsey on 8 August. A procession had then been formed to St John's. On 9 August no fewer than 50,000 people visited the church to pay their respects. The funeral took place on 10 August and involved another procession from Walworth to Nunhead Cemetery, where the scouts were buried. The tragedy made a huge impression at the time. In recent years a booklet by Rex Batten, a researcher on Nunhead Cemetery, has re-awakened interest in the subject on Sheppey and in Southwark.

St Wilfrid's Church, Lorrimore Road, 1960, photographed by the John Ruskin Camera Club. The church was built in 1914–15 to the designs of F.A. Walters, who designed many other Roman Catholic churches, including Ealing Abbey in West London and Buckfast Abbey in Devon. The repairs to St Wilfrid's after wartime bombing are very clear in this picture.

Mrs Pettit, 1893. She was said to be one of the oldest and most faithful members of Pembroke College Mission.

Miss Kate West (standing) and Miss Fanny Langley, two workers at Pembroke College Mission, apparently in the 1890s.

The interior of the basement church at Pembroke College Mission, *c.* 1895. The mission had been founded by members of Pembroke College, Cambridge, in 1885 in the parish of All Saints', Newington. The original buildings were designed by E.S. Prior and were opened in 1892. The mission was one of a large number of such institutions founded by universities and public schools in the late nineteenth century in poor areas to undertake Christian evangelization and voluntary social work. They usually thrived until the First World War. In this case, a new mission church of St Christopher was dedicated in Barlow Street, Walworth, in 1909. After the Second World War very different social and economic conditions, for the givers and the receivers, led to a waning of the movement.

St Mary's Church, Newington Butts, 1873. This building dated from 1792 and was designed by Francis Hurlbatt. Its predecessors had stood on the site from at least the early thirteenth century. Until 1824 there was no other Anglican church in Walworth. It was again rebuilt in 1876, but on a new site in Kennington Park Road, and so the ancient site of Walworth's mother church at the Elephant was vacated.

William Dalrymple Maclagan (1826–1910) was the Rector of St Mary Newington from 1869 to 1876. He rose rapidly in the Church and was appointed Archbishop of York in 1891. He served in that exalted role until 1908.

The interior of St Matthew's Church, New Kent Road, 1927. The church had been built a stone's throw from the Elephant in 1866–7 to the designs of Henry Jarvis. Martin Travers remodelled its interior in the late 1920s. This work was undertaken for Canon T.P. Stevens, who was the energetic vicar from 1924 to 1930.

A fancy-dress party in St Matthew's Church hall in the 1930s.

The interior of St Peter's Church, Liverpool Grove, photographed by A.E. Wade in 1899. St Peter's was built in 1823–5 as one of the first daughter-churches of St Mary Newington, Walworth's ancient parish church. The architect was Sir John Soane, who had designed the Bank of England. St Peter's was built for the Church Building Commissioners, a body formed in 1818 to build churches at Government expense. The style of the Commissioners' early churches was usually Classical. The next generation was to make Gothic once again the normal style for a church.

MILITARY & WARTIME SOUTHWARK

A parade of Boer War Volunteers outside Bermondsey Town Hall, Spa Road, apparently on 22 May 1901. The 1st Service Section of the 3rd Volunteer Battalion, The Queen's (Royal West Surrey Regiment), had gone from Bermondsey to South Africa to fight the Boers in 1900. Upon their return, they were welcomed in the streets of Bermondsey and more formally at the Town Hall. The Town Clerk, Frederick Ryall (seen in the background in wig and gown), read the Bermondsey Borough Council's address. The Mayor at the time, Colonel Samuel Bevington, had commanded the 3rd Volunteer Battalion for many years. It was what we would now call Bermondsey's unit of the Territorial Army.

Officers and NCOs of the 24th Battalion of the London Regiment, *c.* 1912–13. This was Walworth's unit of the Territorial Army and traced its origins to 1860, in response to a supposed threat from the Emperor Napoleon III. The unit was for long known as the 4th Volunteer Battalion, The Queen's (Royal West Surrey Regiment). The uniforms and insignia speak volumes. Standing at the left is Sgt-Major C.M. Barrett. Seated in front of him is Colour-Sgt H.W. Norris. Second from the right at the back is Sgt-Instructor J.T. Davies, who was a prominent figure in many photographs of the regiment. The two officers at the front (with swords) are Lt T.S. Malcolmson (left) and Capt. H.L.F.B. Nadaud (right).

Lance-Corporal Leonard James Keyworth VC is fêted at the Drill Hall in Walworth on 12 July 1915 after his investiture at Buckingham Palace by King George V. Although he came from Lincoln, he served in the 1/24th Battalion of the London Regiment, which was based at the Drill Hall in New Street (later renamed Braganza Street) in Walworth. Keyworth won his VC for an action at Givenchy, near Béthune in northern France, on 25–26 May 1915. He died from wounds on 19 October in the same year, aged 22, and was buried at Abbeville. In 1919 Dantzic Street at the Elephant was renamed Keyworth Street in his honour, and Faunce Street School later became Keyworth School.

During the First World War the 1/24th Battalion of the London Regiment, from Walworth, formed part of the 47th (London) Division on the Western Front. On 28 October 1918 the Band and Drums of the battalion led the division in a ceremonial entry into Lillie in northern France after the retreat of Kaiser Wilhelm's army. Drum-Major W. Mew heads the procession. Posters set up in the city to welcome the division are among the records of the battalion which are now kept in Southwark Local Studies Library.

Damage caused at 113–115 Keeton's Road, Bermondsey, by a Zeppelin raid on 7 September 1915. It is often forgotten that there were air raids on London in the First World War and that their results were all too similar to those of the Blitz in 1940–1, although there were, of course, far fewer raids than in the Second World War. This photograph was taken by R.J. Angel, Bermondsey's Borough Engineer.

This photograph shows that part of Jamaica Road now called Old Jamaica Road, probably in the 1920s. The Drill Hall of Bermondsey's Territorials (22nd London Regiment (The Queen's)) is on the right, and behind it there is the memorial erected after the First World War. The Drill Hall was built by Colonel Samuel Bevington, who commanded the local Volunteers and became Bermondsey's first mayor in 1900. He headed the great leather firm of Bevingtons & Sons in Abbey Street (*see* page 29).

Mrs Gladys Henley receiving farthings from children in War Weapons Week, 1941. Mrs Henley was Mayoress of Bermondsey from 1939 to 1941; her husband, Albert Richard George Henley, the Mayor, had been killed at the Town Hall the week before.

A temporary war memorial was unveiled by the Mayor of Bermondsey, William Bustin, at Mill Pond Bridge, West Lane, Rotherhithe, in 1920. It was dedicated by the Bishop of Southwark, Cyril Forster Garbett (later appointed Archbishop of York). A permanent memorial afterwards took its place and remains there today.

Civil Defence in Bermondsey in the Second World War. This photograph was provided by Mr Daniel Seabrook, who worked under the Medical Officer of Health, Dr D.M. Connan. The Red Cross and St John's Ambulance were fully involved in all the preparations to deal with the Blitz. Here we see stretcher parties and, on the right, a mobile hospital. Many Civil Defence workers were killed or injured during the war.

More Civil Defence workers in wartime Bermondsey. The borough suffered very badly in the Blitz because of its proximity to the heart of London and because of its docks and railway lines. In 1946 James D. Stewart, the Borough Librarian, wrote an account called *Bermondsey in War*, which was published as a booklet in 1980.

ROYAL OCCASIONS

*Queen Juliana of the Netherlands (left) and Queen Elizabeth (right) visit the Time and Talents Settlement,
193 Bermondsey Street, November 1950, in the company of the Mayor of Bermondsey, Eileen Greenwood.
The Mayor is wearing a Dutch medal.*

Queen Victoria's carriage passes the premises of Peter Boswell & Sons in Borough Road, Southwark, on 21 June 1897, in the great procession which marked her Diamond Jubilee. Soldiers of the Queen in their thousands were on parade that day. The unprecedented occasion of a Diamond Jubilee, combined with a sense of material progress and the high noon of Empire, made this celebration a spectacular one. Monuments and mementoes of it appeared all over the country. In Borough Road itself, seats were sold in a stand to raise money for a new library; the building which was erected still stands near St George's Circus, although it is no longer a library. The blacking factory of Day & Martin can be seen in the background: a reminder that Southwark was an important industrial area.

The proclamation of King Edward VII's coronation at Bermondsey Town Hall, Spa Road, 15 July 1901. The Town Clerk of Bermondsey, Frederick Ryall, read the proclamation in the presence of the Mayor, Samuel Bevington, and of several robed aldermen, of whom John Dumphreys is conspicuous on the left with his side-whiskers. Four trumpeters of the 3rd Volunteer Battalion, The Queen's (Royal West Surrey Regiment), blew a fanfare before and after the proclamation. The dignitaries and their guests then repaired to carriages and brakes, which took them successively to Rotherhithe Town Hall and St Olave's Grammar School, where the ceremony was repeated. The civic pride of a new borough and the national pride of Edwardian England were clearly reflected in these observances.

New Street (later Braganza Street) in Walworth is shown *en fête* for the coronation of King Edward VII in 1902. The building with the pediment belonged to the 4th Volunteer Battalion, The Queen's (Royal West Surrey Regiment) (*see* pages 112–114). The Queen of the title was Catherine of Braganza, the wife of King Charles II. Her marriage brought Tangier into English ownership, and a regiment therefore had to be raised to provide a garrison.

A 'King's Dinner' in Bermondsey, 5 July 1902. King Edward VII had set aside £30,000 to provide dinner for half a million poor Londoners, to mark his coronation. This is one of the forty-three dinners arranged in Bermondsey for a total of 22,000 people. Although the dinners took place as scheduled, the coronation had to be postponed because of the King's appendicitis. It was re-arranged later in the year.

Southwark Central Library in the Walworth Road and Southwark Town Hall (to the left) decorated for the coronation of King Edward VII in 1902. The library had been built in 1893 and the town hall had been opened as Newington Vestry Hall in 1865. It was in this coronation year that Henry Syer Cuming's collection was bequeathed to the Metropolitan Borough of Southwark. A gallery was then built at the back of Southwark Central Library to house it. The museum opened there in 1906.

The Southwark municipal contingent waiting outside Borough Road Library to welcome King George V and Queen Mary, 30 July 1910. The King, who had succeeded to the throne less than three months earlier, drove in semi-state through East and South London, taking in Borough High Street, Borough Road and Westminster Bridge Road. The Mayor of Southwark in this picture is Canon J.W. Horsley (1845–1921), who was also Rector of St Peter's Church, Walworth, from 1894 to 1911. He was a very energetic priest and wrote a number of books on social issues of the day.

The Mayors of the South London boroughs and their wives wait outside the former Vestry Hall of the Parish of St George the Martyr, Southwark, in Borough Road to meet King George V and Queen Mary during their coronation drive on 23 June 1911. Next to the lamp on the left can be seen the shield of arms of the Metropolitan Borough of Southwark; and the next shield along is that of the Metropolitan Borough of Bermondsey, showing a ship (for Rotherhithe), an axe (for St Olave's) and a lion with a crozier (for Bermondsey Abbey).

Derrick Street, Rotherhithe, whose usual dreary aspect was transformed for the Silver Jubilee of King George V in 1935.

A children's street party in Guy Street, Bermondsey, which was held to mark King George V's Silver Jubilee.

BRITAIN IN OLD PHOTOGRAPHS

To order any of these titles please telephone our distributor, Littlehampton Book Services on 01903 721596
For a catalogue of these and our other titles please ring Regina Schinner on 01453 731114